THE NIGHT BEFORE SERIES™

The Night Before Columbus Sailed on the Sea

Written by: Timothy Penland
Illustrated by: Kayee Au

cane creek publishers

dawson media®

'Twas the night before Columbus
Sailed on the sea,
He had this grand plan
and tomorrow he'd leave.

The century was fourteen
The year ninety two
And Columbus believed
Some thoughts that were new.

Back then most men thought
That the world must be flat.
If you came to the edge
You'd fall off and go "splat."

But now some were saying,
The earth was a ball,
You'd not come to an edge
So you just couldn't fall.

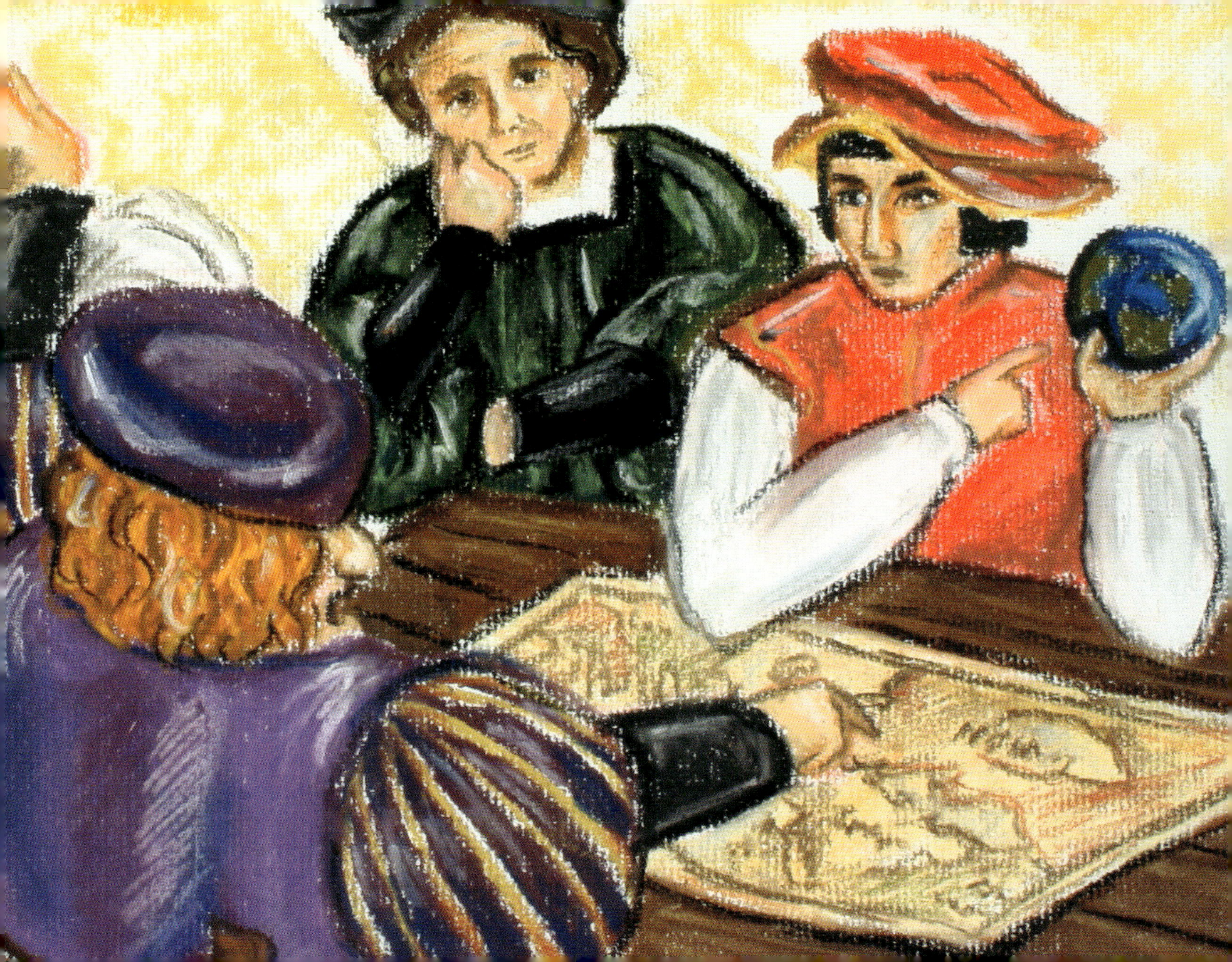

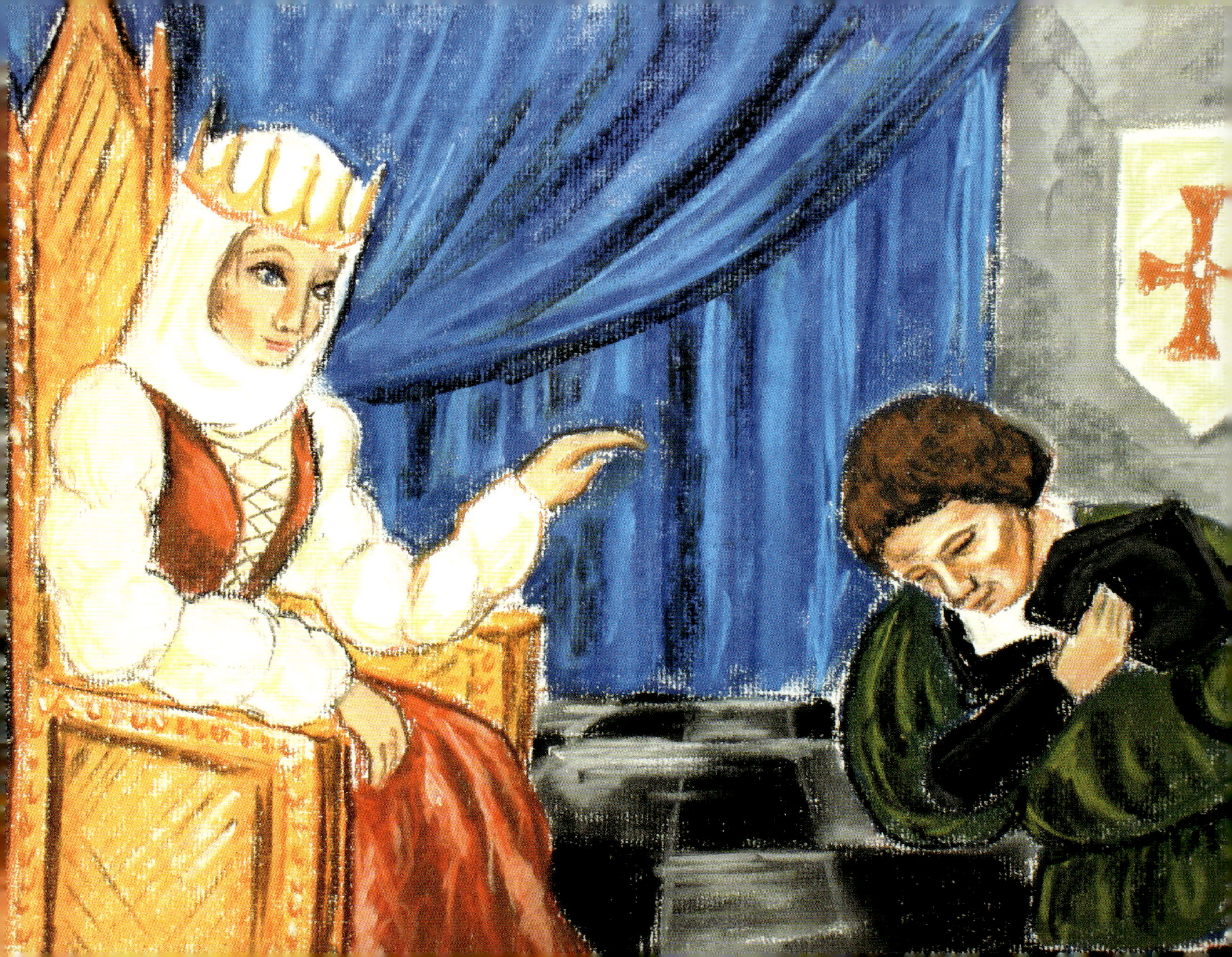

Isabella the queen
Would help this brave man
She thought he was right
She believed in his plan.

She was queen over Spain
and backed his idea,
with the Nina, the Pinta,
and the Santa Maria.

He just didn't know
"How long was the trip?"
So he'd loaded and loaded
Those three little ships.

Those ships he had filled
With all kinds of things
From food to weapons
To clothing to rings.

Once they were loaded
and the men all aboard
Columbus sat down
And prayed to his Lord.

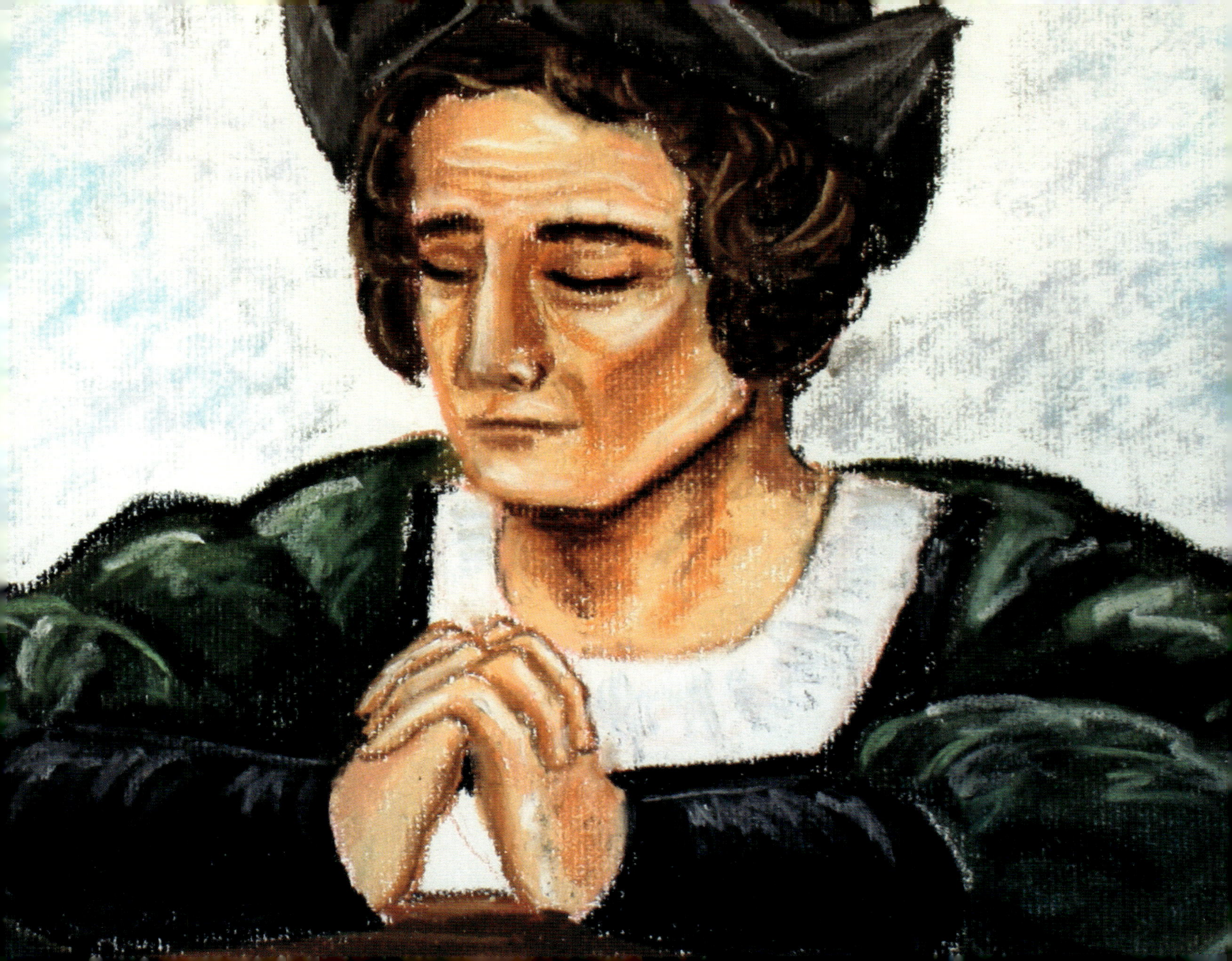

Men had proven that Asia,
was off to the east,
and returned with great tales,
of its people and beasts.

So Columbus had reasoned
If earth really was round
He'd sail to the west
And see what he found.

He set sail the next day
Toward where the sun set
He said he would go
'til Asia he met.

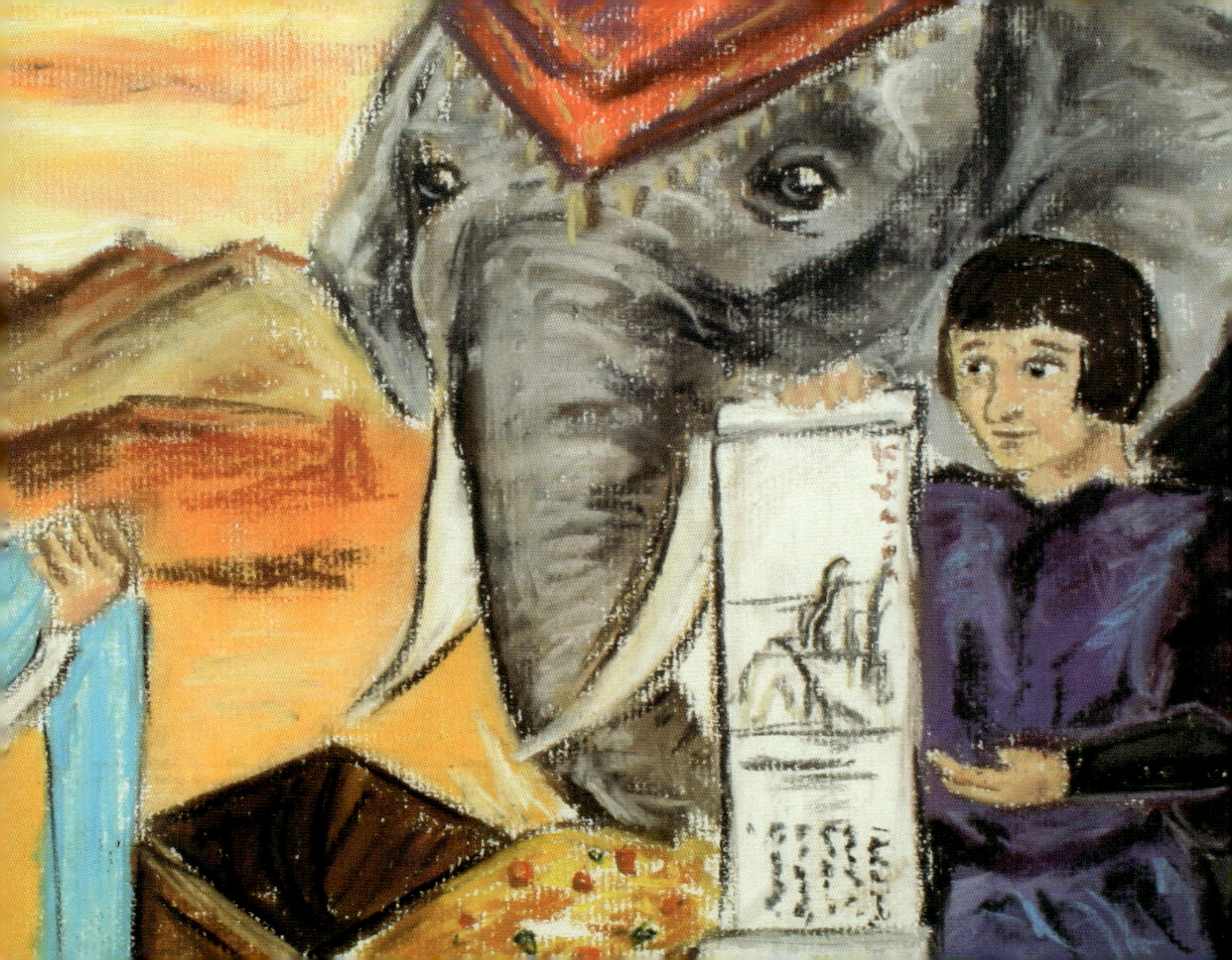

They sailed and they sailed
Days upon days
But out to the West
They saw nothing but haze.

Some sailors decided
Their leader was "mad,"
But he told them, "Be patient,
There's wealth to be had!"

"If we can just find
A new way to the East
We'll all be rich men
Even those who are least."

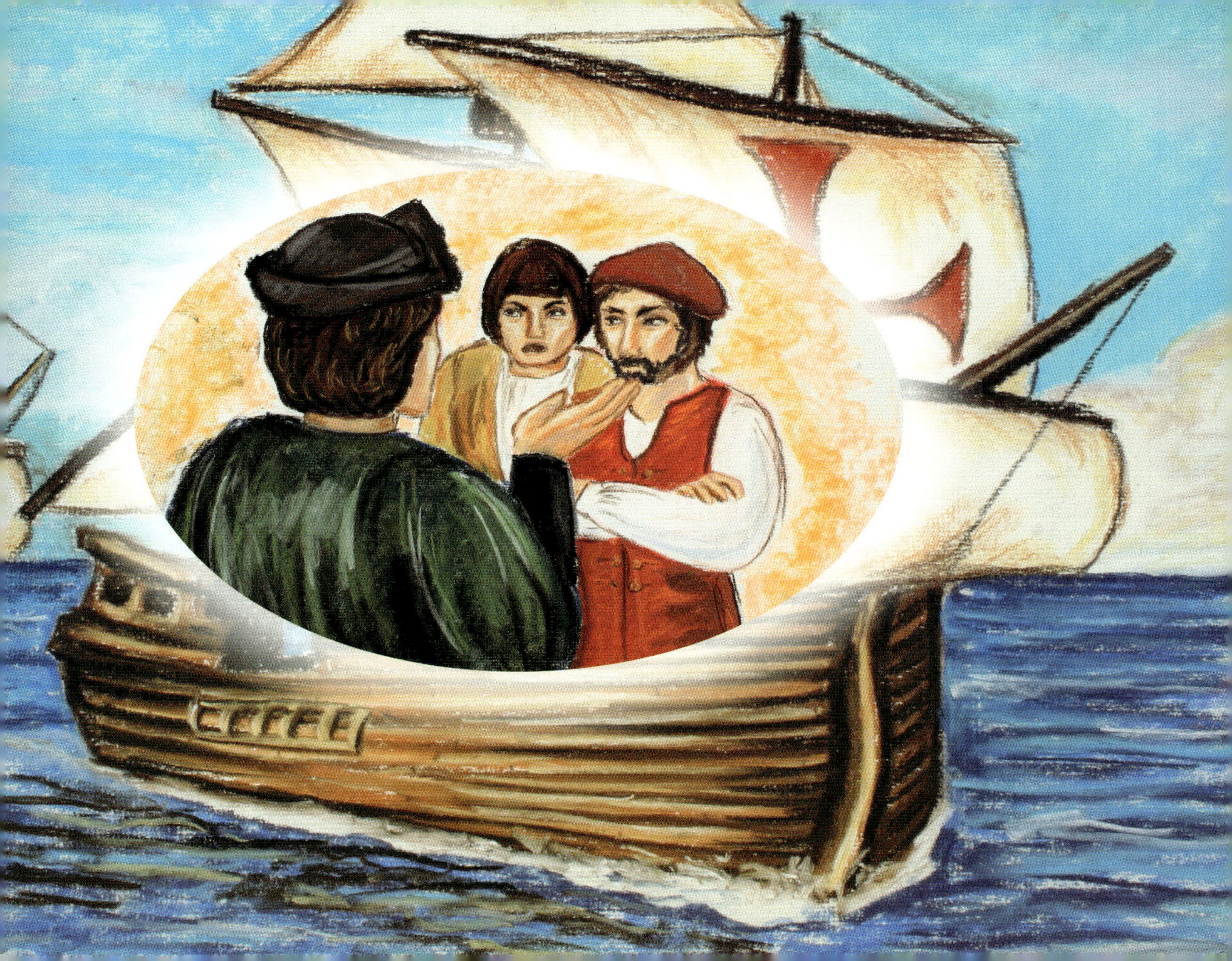

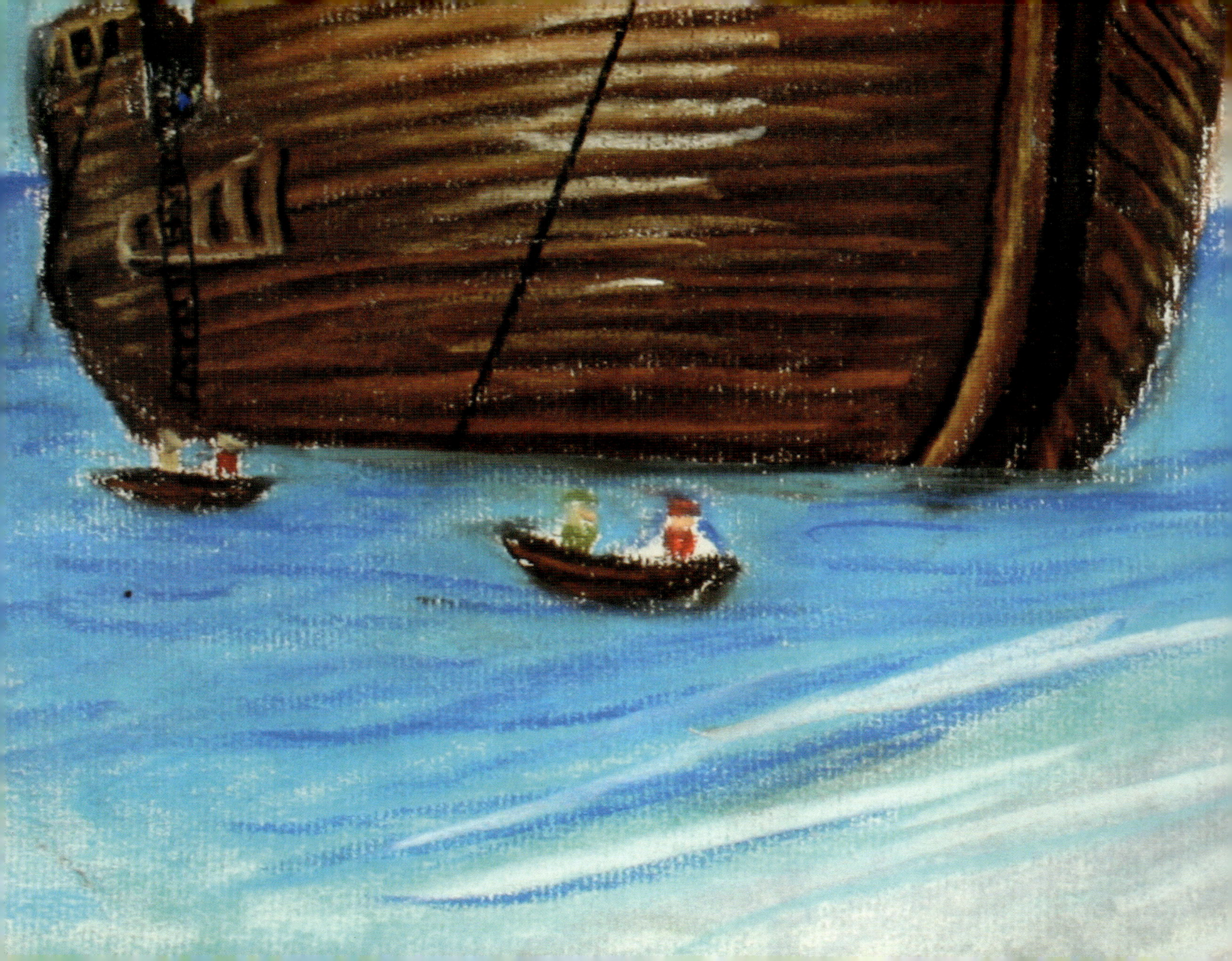

Then one day they saw
In the distance some land
They knew in no time
They'd be standing on sand.

The anchors were set
Just short of the surf,
Then small boats were used,
To row to the turf.

Search parties were sent
To check out the place,
They discovered some men
but not of their race.

Columbus was sure
They'd found India's coast
The people were Indians
Later he'd boast.

He had no way of knowing
That he stood on the ground
Of a rather large island
In a "New World" he'd found.

He was quite disappointed
'cause he just couldn't see
This trip was historic
Or how famous he'd be.

Others would follow
And find many things
Along with great peoples
Their chiefs and their kings.

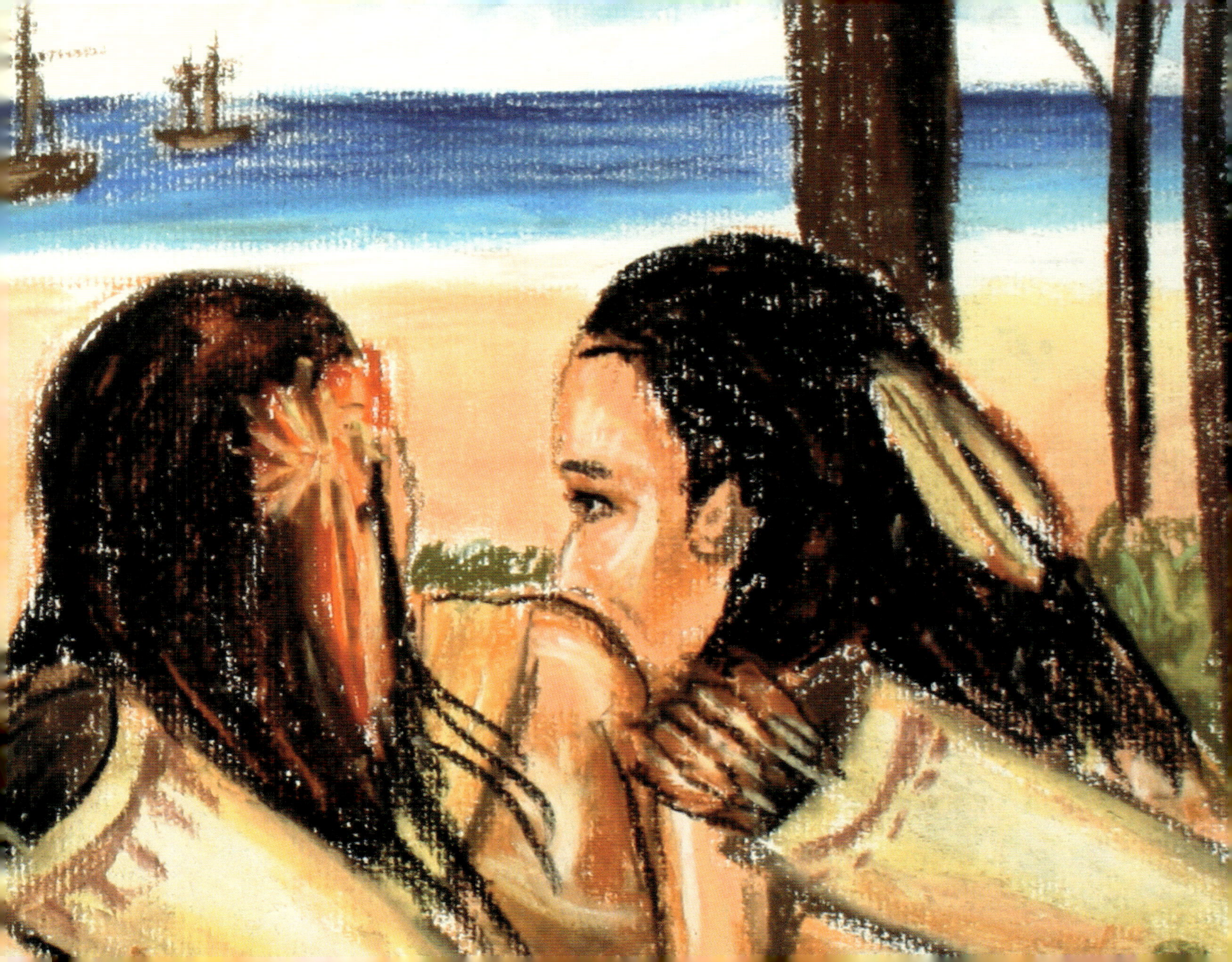

America is what
We call it today
If Columbus could see it
Who knows what he'd say.

'Cause millions of people
Now live in this place
From all over the world
And from every race.

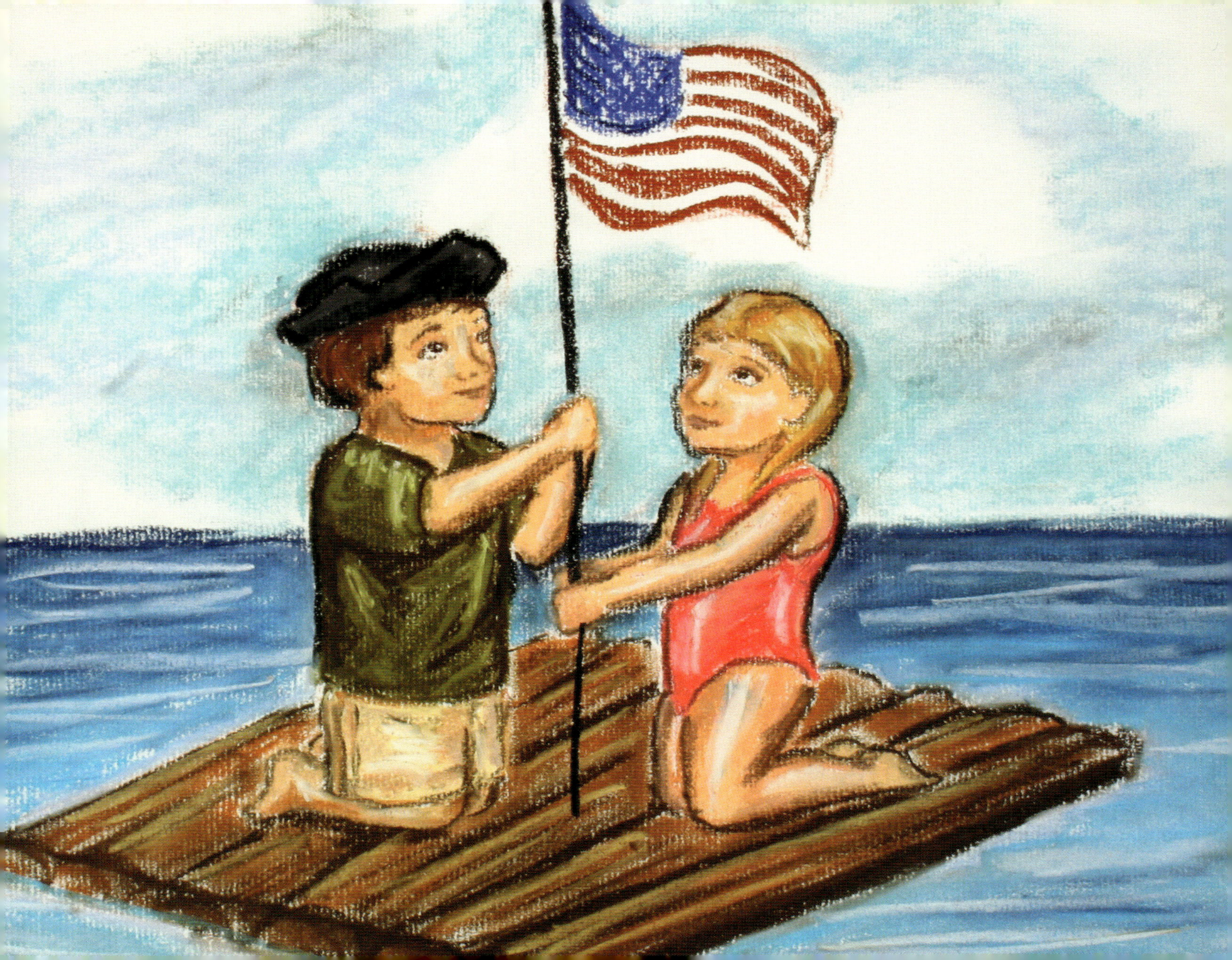

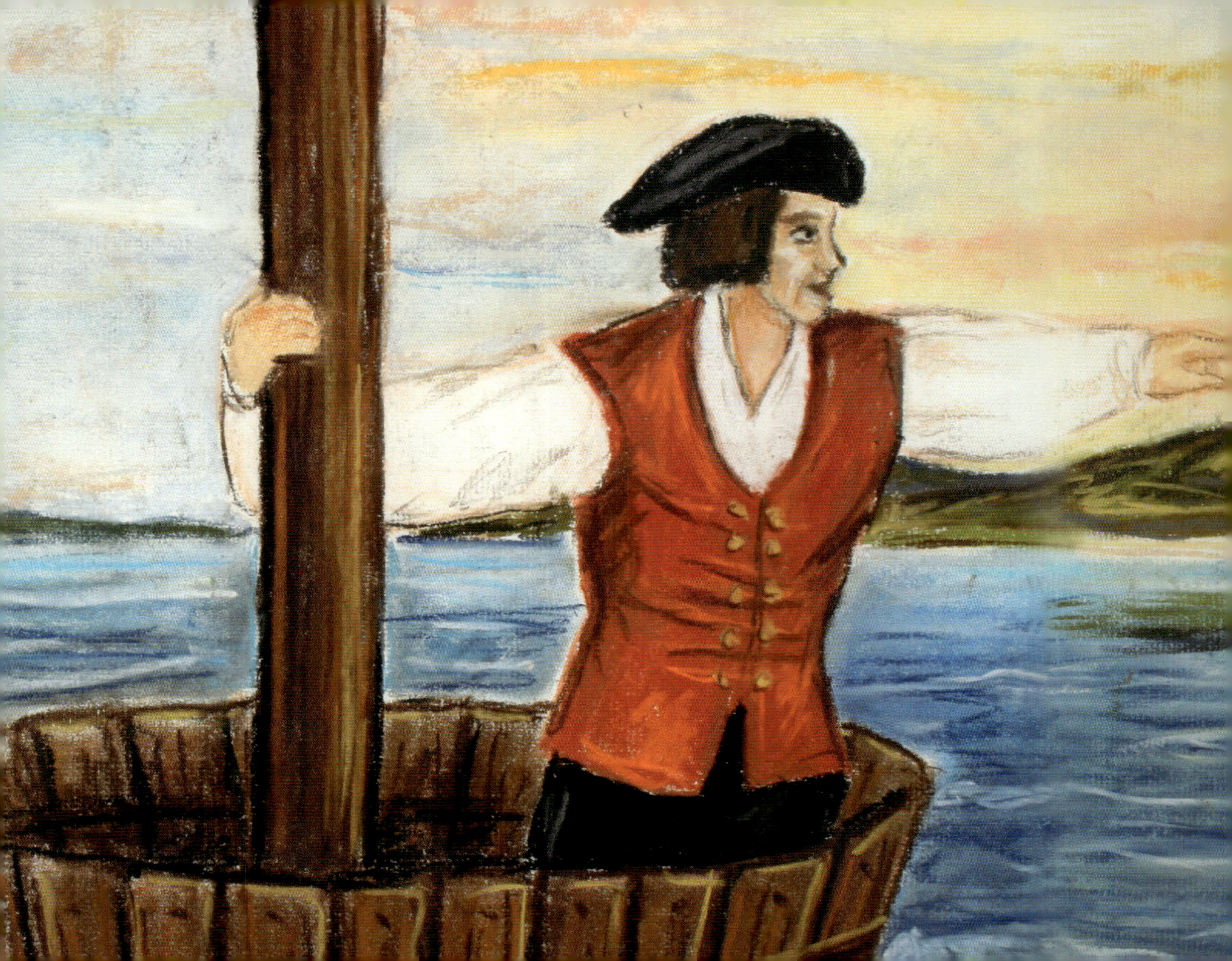

It's been 500 years
Since Columbus set sail
He stuck to his dream
He just wouldn't fail.

His brave exploration
Was the first step of many
That would one day result
In this great land of plenty.

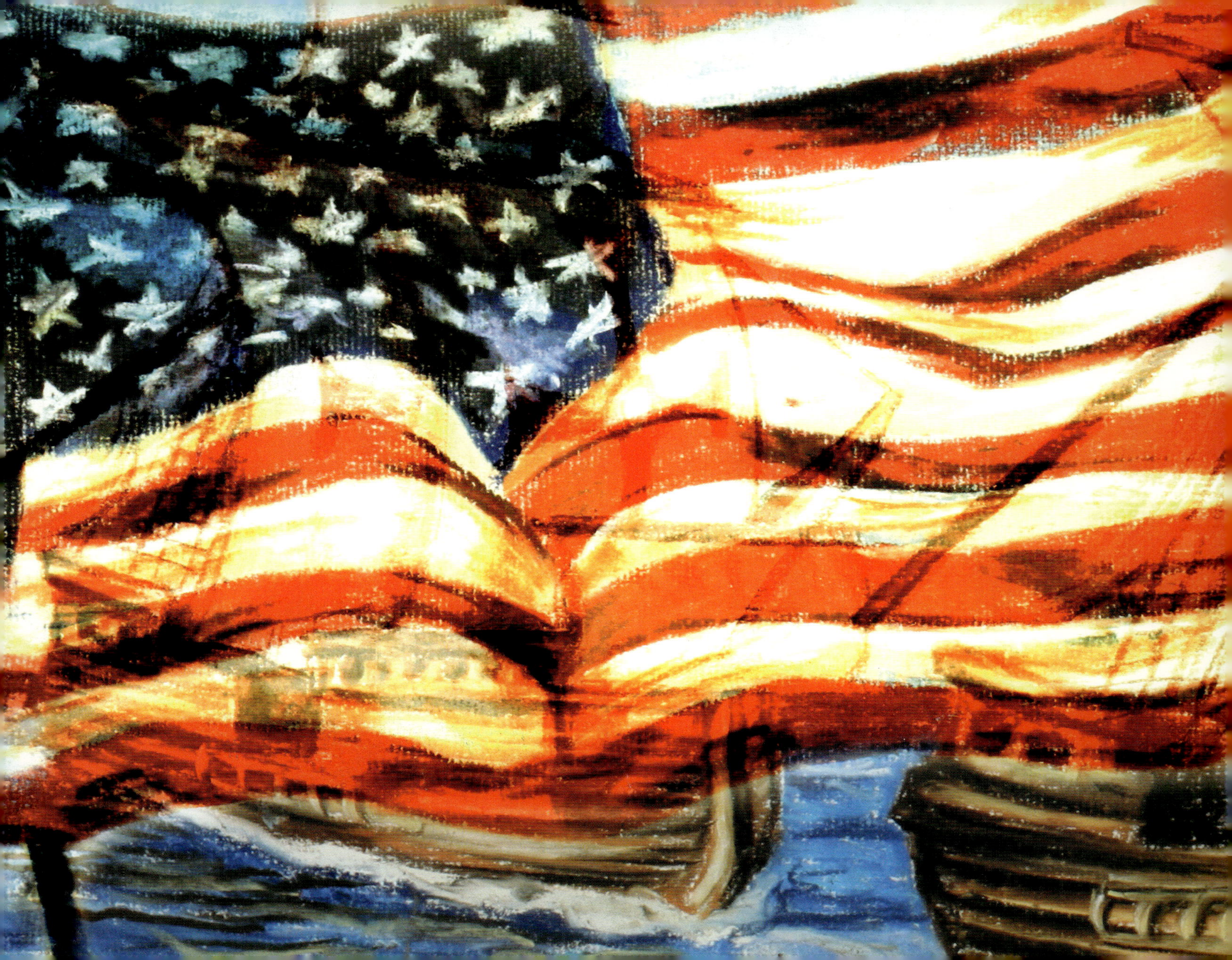

The voyage of Columbus
Is important today
For its part of the tale
Of the U-S of A.

This book is dedicated to Elizabeth, my wonderful granddaughter. Her inquisitive spirit and bright smile are ample incentive to make sure that the wonderful history of our nation is passed on to a new generation.

Acknowledgements

The amazing illustrations are the work of Kayee Au. Kayee has been a joy to work with and has a unique insight into the stories I have attempted to relate. Special thanks go to Frank and Huey Min Au, - Kayee's parents whose support and encouragement have been immeasurably important. Thanks to Angie and Brett for introducing me to Kayee.

The Creative group at Cane Creek Publishers who has brought this work to life - Joy, Ben, and Kirk have each added their magical and imaginative skills. Special thanks to brother Jon who first gave me the idea of beginning this series of American history books.

Timothy Penland

© 2010 by Timothy Penland

All rights reserved. No part of this publication may be reproduced in any form without written permission from Dawson Media, 3820 N. 30th Street, Colorado Springs, CO 80904. www.DawsonMedia.com

Dawson Media and the Dawson Media logo are registered trademarks of NavPress. Absence of ® in connection with marks of Dawson Media or other parties does of indicate an absence of registration of those marks.

ISBN: 978-1-93565-102-4

Library of Congress Control Number: 2010923114

Illustrations by Kayee Au
Cover and Interior Design by Kirk Hawkins

Printed in India

1 2 3 4 5 6 7 8 / 14 13 12 11 10